AS INTENSE AS IT GETS, IT'S JUST

TURBULENCE

CW00763484

AS INTENSE AS IT GETS, IT'S JUST

TURBULENCE

MASTER THE FIVE TOOLS OF
A.T.L.A.S TO NAVIGATE ANY STORM
& REMAP YOUR LIFE

© 2025 Jo Swann

All rights reserved.
No part of this publication may be reproduced, stored in a retrieval
system, or transmitted in any form or by any means whether
electronic, mechanical, photocopying, recording, or otherwise
without the prior written permission of the publisher.

ISBN 978-1-0369-0538-5

First Edition, February 2025

This book is a work of nonfiction. It reflects the author's personal experiences
and insights. The information in this book is provided for informational purposes
only and is not intended as a substitute for professional advice. The author and
publisher disclaim any liability in connection with the use of this information.

Cover design, all images and graphics by Jo Swann

Published by Hansah Life™
www.hansahlife.com

To my Mum and Dad, for your unwavering, unconditional love and support. Never fading, even through my most turbulent years. You've always encouraged, guided, and inspired me to find my wings.

To my brothers, who may never take my advice but will read this book out of sheer sibling loyalty.

To my sister, my confidante and best friend, who knows just when to lift me up and when to let me fly free.

And to my husband, whose love and support, amidst the ever-changing skies, provide me with the freedom to journey and the safe haven to return to when I need it most.

To all my family and friends, whose love, encouragement, and shared presence on this journey have made every wingbeat possible.

Thank you, all of you, for being my companions in this adventure.

A.T.L.A.S

FIVE MIND TOOLS TO NAVIGATE
ANY STORM & RE-MAP YOUR LIFE

Imagine yourself with mental tools that instantly shift your state of mind, allowing you to effortlessly manage anxiety, overwhelm and life's challenges. Picture yourself equipped with frameworks that make changing habits easy.

Envision connecting with your own body intelligence to guide you in re-mapping your life according to your true desires, free from the constraints of conditioning and social norms

This book presents practical, effective tools you can use in the heat of the moment. They empower you to face life's storms head-on, rise above turbulence to gain clarity and know when to take shelter and rest. For those in search of purpose, these tools unveil a profound source of trust and connection.

Like a butterfly adapting to atmospheric changes, A.T.L.A.S. helps you attune to your inner self and the world around you, providing tools to navigate through life's turbulence.

A.T.L.A.S

Awareness of self

You have squeezed yourself into the narrow frame of a perceived individual. Now what are you going to do about that?

Thoughts & feelings

How do you decide which thoughts and feelings to pay attention to and which ones to ignore?

Locus of control

What keeps you trapped? Could it be blaming what you can't change?

Adventurous awakening

You have no idea what you are capable of, so stop fighting for your limitations.

Sense of abundance

What if tapping into nature could manifest your greatest desires?

CONTENTS

"A human being is part of a whole, called by us the "Universe," a part limited in time and space.

He experiences himself, his thoughts and feelings, as something separated from the rest. A kind of optical delusion of his consciousness.

This delusion is a kind of prison for us, restricting us to our personal desires and to affection for a few persons nearest us.

Our task must be to free ourselves from this prison by widening our circles of compassion to embrace all living creatures and the whole of nature in its beauty." – Albert Einstein

PROLOGUE

FACING THE STORM

Why Your Past Isn't The Problem
But Your Approach Might Be

It was a beautiful June morning in the tropics as I set out for my usual early morning run. Sometimes I listen to music, and sometimes I listen to a podcast. Today was a podcast day. I'm a fan of Jonny Wilkinson, the former professional rugby player. I will never forget his heart-stopping, game-winning drop goal in the 2003 Rugby World Cup. I once helped organise his Mount Kinabalu climb adventure, so I feel a special connection to him.

On this June morning, I listened to his interview with Rupert Spira, a teacher of non-duality.

A wave of goosebumps rippled across my body, and the hairs on my arms stood on end. Something profound stirred deep within me. I felt a shift. What did this mean? Could it be the resolution to decades of spiritual exploration? For years, I had sensed a common thread running through all religions and spiritual teachings. I'd come to realise that these enlightened beings were describing their experiences as best they could, shaped by the time and place in which they lived. Yet, over centuries, their teachings had been taken literally,

"If we were to distil into a single sentence all the spiritual teachings from the last 3,000 years, we would arrive at a simple understanding: Peace and happiness are the nature of our being, and we share our being with everyone and everything." – Rupert Spira

altered, and endlessly reinterpreted. Rupert's words cut through this complexity, offering the simplicity I had been searching for. Since that day in June, I've devoted much of my time to studying this concept, which ultimately inspired the first tool in this book.

This is not a spiritual book; I'm not here to convince you of anything. On the contrary, this small book is practical and experience based. These tools work for me daily. They work for my clients daily. They work when your life pivots, they empower you to do what you say you want to do and if you don't know what you want to do, they will guide the way.

They are action tools; they will help you create your own navigation path for a life of wonderful experiences!

Most people think that we are not adequately equipped for this human experience full of struggle and challenge. The truth is, we have everything we need within us, we have just forgotten the coordinates and misplaced our internal compass.

The very fact that we are human beings, distinguished by advanced cognitive abilities, emotional complexity, and the capacity for abstract reasoning, language, and culture means that we will inevitably experience trauma.

This trauma can range from acute to chronic, even deeply visceral. While I recognise that traumatic events and experiences are extremely challenging, they also carry lessons and opportunities for growth. With the right tools, they can become powerful teachers.

Traditional therapy often focuses on a person's past experiences and trauma. This approach can take years to yield positive outcomes, often providing only temporary relief, and I believe that dwelling on the past can amplify its power. I don't place heavy emphasis on childhood developmental processes, attachment histories, or significant past events as the primary causes of current issues. However, they are very good indicators of where we may have started to get lost, negative childhood experiences will often be the catalyst for us beginning to design our limiting mental constructs.

While it can be helpful to understand *why* our problems exist and where our coping mechanisms come from, real change requires a different focus. To transform these patterns, we must examine how the problem is manifesting in the present and what current mechanisms are sustaining it.

In other words, I explore "how and when people generate their problems". I help clients develop distinction strategies and I teach them new skills that enable them to change their inner state immediately. Once released from the immediate discomfort of the situation, we can use our brain to work with us and not against us, to implement new ways of showing up in the world, which form a vital part of the treatment.

Nobody has ever come to therapy to "change" the past, that's impossible. People come to therapy to change the future.

When I begin working with someone, whether it's for anxiety, depression, dependency, or poor health choices, I start by examining how they manage their thoughts, feelings, beliefs, and perceptions. Typically, the first question I ask is, "How do you decide which thoughts you pay attention to and which ones you ignore?"

At this point, a blank expression typically crosses their face as they try to recall the process. After a few seconds, they look up with a puzzled gaze, "I don't !" That's when I know I can help them!

This small book will provide you with a set of five tools that will help you. I've called it my A.T.L.A.S. because, not only are these tools valuable individually, but together they will help you remap your navigation route, empowering you to create the life you want to live. This map will connect you to a source of unlimited potential. A powerful source that you will learn is a place to come from and return to.

What this book will not do is take away life's challenges and struggles. The pendulum will always swing between joy and heartache, good and bad, fair and unfair, hard and easy.

These tools will help shift your perspective on the dark clouds you face, so you no longer fear them. They will guide you when the path ahead seems unclear. You'll learn when to seek shelter and wait out the storm, and when to rise above the turbulence, where the sun always shines, and the sky is clear. You'll discover that clarity isn't always necessary when you have the right navigation tools. Most importantly, you'll realise that you already possess all the answers you need for your unique journey.

We dive deep. It's thought-provoking. If you can't follow everything right away, don't worry, stay with it. In each chapter, I summarise the main points as key takeaways and explain the tools in a simple way. I encourage you to pay full attention because if anything resonates with you in this first chapter, then welcome aboard. You're on a journey. It will be bumpy, but those bumps are just turbulence and what you begin to realise is, the turbulence makes us stronger. Trust the tools.

I also want to share that these tools have worked for me during incredibly challenging times and moments when hope seemed out of reach.

These tools have helped countless others with dependency, binge eating, anxiety, overwhelm, habit change, and health and fitness goals. They have made dreams come true. They have transformed people's lives. I use them every day, they grow with us.

Take what you need and make it yours.

Clarifying Key Terms

Words are powerful and hold different meanings for different people, so let's define how I am using various words. You might find it helpful to substitute

these words for alternatives that are more meaningful to you.

The Mind: The lens from which and in which we experience the world around us and within us. A combina-
tion of perception (sight, sound, touch, smell, taste)
plus thought.

The Brain: Highly complex organ. The command centre
for our central nervous system.

The Body: Our physical body, made up of all our organs, flesh, skeletons, muscles etc.

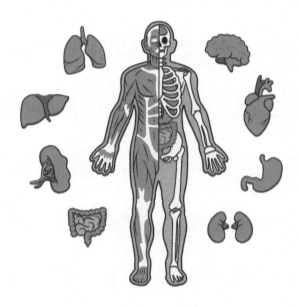

The Ego: A sense of self that arises from the identification with thoughts, feelings, and perceptions. It is a construct, an image we create through our experiences and conditioning, forming a narrative about who we believe we are.

Awareness: The whole, unlimited, infinite, nature. Other words for this include, spirit, higher power, true self, true being, universe, source, god, consciousness.

*Self-awareness is self-destruction –
and that's a good thing!*

WARNING
This book will dissolve your sense of self.
Side effects may include
uncontrollable freedom
and spontaneous enlightenment.

CHAPTER ONE

AWARENESS OF SELF-PERCEIVED LIMITATION VS INFINITE POTENTIAL

"You have squeezed yourself into the narrow frame of a perceived individual. Now what are you going to do about that?"

Do you ever feel there is a "you" beyond the surface "you"? This deeper "you" has always been there, unchanging and ageless. This presence has remained the same as far back as you can remember. It was there when you were 10 years old, 15 years old, 25 years old, and it remains the same today. When you connect with this "you," it becomes an observer of your thoughts, feelings, and everything that comes at you through your senses.

At first, you might refer to this "you" as the mind, but there is a persistent feeling that there is more to this "you" than just a mind. While calling it the mind might seem satisfying, it leaves many questions unanswered. Some people refer to this "you" as consciousness, spirit, higher source, or being, which I suggest is closer to the truth.

Some spiritual teachers call this "you" the "I AM" before anything is attributed. I call it my "true self" or "true nature"," and I invite you to call it whatever you choose.

You might be wondering why this recognition of our "true self" or true being is so important. Good question!

Without this recognition, we mistakenly identify ourselves as a separate self, a limited being burdened with our thoughts, feelings, and perceptions. This can be overwhelming, disempowering, and hopeless, making us feel lost and help-less to effect powerful change.

The separate self is a mental construct that we have created with words. An image created through our experiences and conditioning, many of them sub-conscious. This separate self, often referred to as the ego, is an illusion. Which is not to say it doesn't exist; it exists but is not what it appears to be.

Once you become aware of your true self and spend time connecting with this deeper part of you, you begin to experience the infinite, boundless, timeless power within. Just like any new tool you discover, you must learn how to use your true self properly to experience its full value. The more you engage with your true self, the better it performs. Your true self doesn't communi-cate with words; it's not rational in the conventional sense. You must learn a new way to converse with this inner essence—a dialogue of intuition and feeling, a language beyond words that promises a more profound understanding of yourself and the world around you.

Fabulous, you might say! But how is this newfound awareness of true self actually going to help when I need it most?

Let's first explore the underlying nature, in other words the essence or substance of the true self, which is inherently free from the content of all experience (thoughts, feelings and perception).

I love the simple reflection of deep sleep.

Close your eyes and recall a time when you woke up knowing you had a terrific night's sleep. Do you remember that feeling of deep restfulness? How did that feel? Take a moment and write down what you felt.

NOTES

"Is deep sleep the absence of awareness or the awareness of absence?" – Rupert Spira

You may have written down emotions such as contentment, peace, love, safety, happiness, and relaxation. Deep sleep is the closest we get to experiencing the nature of the true self due to the complete absence of thinking, sensing, and perceiving. That feeling you have upon waking from deep sleep is the pure knowingness of self.

Meditation is a powerful way to connect with our true self. The mind always wants something to focus on, so during meditation, we might direct our attention towards an object of experience, such as a sound, sight (a candle), feeling, or breath. We do this to steady our mind and minimise the content of experience (our thoughts and perceptions) to create space, space between thoughts, space between stimulus and response, space to start observing our thoughts and questioning their validity, questioning our limiting beliefs. When we quiet the conscious mind and connect with our true self, our authentic nature, we open the door to new possibilities.

Once we connect, the knowing of our own being, our true self is undeniable, and we can be absolutely certain that this is the most secure and fulfilling experience there is. When we face challenges, the recognition of our true self can bring profound comfort and clarity. Our true being is analogous to the clear, calm blue sky in which the turbulent clouds of our thoughts and emotions form and disperse. Our true self is complete, we are complete.

Demystifying Mysticism

I, like many people, used to think that enlightenment or awakening was some extraordinary mystical experience that one attained, as a result of effort, discipline and years of practice. What I came to realise through various teachers such as Rupert Spira, Eckhart Tolle, Mooji and others is that enlightenment is in-fact a fancy name for the awareness or recognition of our true self, or true being. Not the being that we might become if we practise hard enough, but the being that each of us is now, but which we do not see clearly, because of its entanglement with the content of experience and our ego.

For the vast majority of us, this awakening or enlightenment is actually quite boring as far as feelings go and instead of a sudden realisation it can come as a gradual understanding that peace and happiness are the nature of our true being and we share our being with everyone and everything. Living from this place however is not boring at all, it's profoundly life changing.

Key Takeaways

Here's how this knowledge helps navigate the storm:

Inner Stability:
When difficulties arise, they often stir up fear, rage, anxiety, hopelessness and confusion. By recognising that our true self is the calm, ever-present awareness behind these thoughts and feelings, we find a stable place within us that remains untouched by life's challenges. We can therefore at any time connect and return to this place for comfort, peace, joy and strength.

Reduced Suffering:
Suffering comes from identifying with the content of experience: thoughts, feelings, and perceptions. From this, we construct a separate self, an "ego," which we believe defines who we are. We create mental constructs and primordial prisons. Understanding that

the content of experience is just temporary appearances on the surface of our being allows us to see them for what they are: fleeting and not defining our true selves, like storm clouds in the clear sky.

Empowerment:

When we understand that we are infinite, boundless, timeless, indivisible consciousness, we realise that we have an immense inner resource to draw from. This connection empowers us, aligning our ambitions with universal consciousness, leading to increased support, synchronicities, and a sense of unity with others.

Shared Being and Interconnectedness:

Understanding that everyone and everything shares the same true being reveals a fundamental interconnectedness behind the appearance of diversity.

This means that even when things appear overwhelming, we can take a moment to remember and connect to our true nature. We can find solace in the fact that the essence of who we are is always untouched, always at peace, limitless and always free. When we connect with this we feel at peace, we feel calm, hopeful and empowered. Just as we do in deep sleep, when our challenges only re-enter our consciousness upon waking.

Whilst this shift in perspective doesn't necessarily change the outer situation, it transforms our experience of it which is the first step. Enlightenment is the beginning, not the end, let's learn how to integrate this knowledge.

POWERFUL TOOL:
Awareness Anchor – Unveiling Your True Self

Introduction

Our true self is often obscured by what we mistakenly identify as our "self," the ego that arises from our mental and emotional experiences. These experiences include our thoughts, images, feelings, sensations, perceptions, activities, and relationships. The Awareness Anchor is a powerful tool designed to lift this veil and reveal our true essence.

Preparation

- Find a quiet, comfortable space where you won't be disturbed.

- If you're driving or engaged in an activity requiring attention, return to this exercise later.

- For an audio guide, scan the QR code provided in your book.

The Practice

Step 1: Centering

- Sit comfortably and close your eyes.

- Take a few deep breaths, allowing yourself to relax fully.

- Let go of any tension or preoccupations.

Step 2: Awareness of Experience

- Ask yourself: "What is it that is aware of my experience right now?"

- Notice any sounds, thoughts, smells, or feelings present.

- Become aware of these experiences, but recognise they are not your core self, you continue to have the sense of being aware of these sounds, thoughts, smells or feelings.

- Observe that these experiences are subjective and transient.

- Reflect: These are what we leave behind when we sleep, so they can't be essential to who we are.

Step 3: Investigating the Self

- Now set aside all content of experience: thoughts, feelings, perceptions, sensations.

- Ask yourself: "If I am not my thoughts, feelings, perceptions, or sensations, what am I?"

- Turn your attention away from the content of experience towards the knower or "observer" of the experience. Towards that which is aware of the experiences.

- This observer is your essential true self, the awareness of your true being.

- Note: This recognition might be fleeting at first. That's perfectly normal.

Step 4: Connecting with Your True Nature

- Recognize that this essential self – the knowing of what you are before experience colours it – is your true self, your true nature and the direct path to peace and happiness.

- Visualise it as the blue sky within which turbulent clouds (your thoughts and experiences) appear and disappear.

Making It a Habit

- Repeat this short investigation daily, even for just one minute.

- Aim for three times a day – perhaps before or after meals.

- Over time, you'll be naturally drawn to this state without setting aside specific time.

- This practice will become a resting place for you, you may return to this place of quiet peace and comfort any time you choose.

As you strengthen your connection to your true self, your thoughts and feelings will begin to change, you'll experience more peace and contentment, you'll gain a deeper understanding of your essential nature.

Remember, this is a journey of self-discovery. Be patient and kind to yourself as you practise the Awareness Anchor.

The Case Of Adrian

When I first began working with Adrian, he was very reactive. His relationships with friends, family, and colleagues often ended in arguments and conflict. Adrian quickly got caught up in what was happening around him. He was dichotomous in his thinking; if you didn't agree with him, you were wrong, and he let you know.

Fortunately, Adrian wanted to make positive changes. He saw that his behaviour would lead to a lonely existence and came to me for help.

Using the "Awareness Anchor" tool from A.T.L.A.S. profoundly changed Adrian's life. This tool taught him to pause in the heat of the moment, allowing him to step back from immediate reactions and observe his emotions without judgement. By anchoring his awareness, he could shift his focus from the turbulent "grey clouds" to his "blue-sky" nature, a state of calm, an alternative perspective.

In his words, "Fewer and fewer experiences have the capacity to upset me. Sure, I have cloudy days, and I find myself in the centre of the storm, but I know it will pass. I know I have the tools and the map to navigate my way out of it."

The Awareness Anchor helped Adrian realise that he is not his fleeting thoughts, feelings, or sensations, but rather the observer of these experiences. This understanding led him to a state of inner peace, transforming his interactions and relationships, and ultimately guiding him toward a more fulfilling, conscious life.

CHAPTER TWO

THOUGHTS & FEELINGS –
RE-ACTION VS ACTION

"Your suffering is a choice,
not a consequence"

How do you decide which thoughts and feelings to pay attention to and which ones to ignore?

Almost all human suffering results from our attachment to thoughts, feelings, perceptions and the mental constructs that we imprison ourselves within. In Chapter One, we brought awareness to the illusory separate self that arises from this attachment, we called it the "ego." Through our investigation, we unveiled our true self, a resting place within us free from the content of our experience and we established a direct path to peace and happiness, to inner completeness, which is a very powerful tool.

At this stage, we have not attempted to challenge, change, or fix our thoughts, feelings, beliefs, and perceptions. We have let them come and go, and observed them. Now, we want a powerful tool to help us manage them effectively.

We Create Our Own Reality

As human beings, we experience life through our own internal representation of the world, informed by our five primary senses: sight, sound, touch, smell, and

"You are unique – just like everyone else. Although each person is unique as an individual, the problems that individuals present for therapy are not all that unique. Each individual has their own reasons for, and ways of suffering. The paths of human suffering that people follow, their symptomatic sequences or processes are well worn and usually plainly visible." – Dr. Michael Yapko, PhD

taste. Beyond these primary senses, there are several additional senses found in other species across the animal kingdom, such as electroreception, magnetoreception, and many more that create different interpretations of reality that are species dependent. How we interpret the world, in other words our "reality", is very different from a dog, a bat, or a whale's world. Reality is therefore extremely subjective, not only as human beings but also as individual human beings.

Believing that our reality is truth, we project our representation onto others and assume another's representation onto ourselves, all the while making judgements, building stories, and catastrophising outcomes.

Our thoughts and feelings arise from how we perceive the world, and how we perceive the world largely determines how happy, healthy, and content we are. This is supported by neuroscience, as we can study the brain's function and observe how different perceptions create different emotional and physical responses. How we perceive the world is so vastly subjective, it is no wonder we experience so much suffering and so many problems.

Feelings often feel undeniably real, and many times they are, yet they arise as the result of the thoughts we form through the lens of our perceptions, shaped by the beliefs and "truths" we assume to be reality. Feelings are significant, and I am not suggesting they should ever be dismissed. No one has the right to tell you that your feelings are not real. However, it is up to each of us to embark on an internal investigation, distinguishing whether the beliefs and perceptions underpinning those feelings are true, real, and valid.

> "Feelings are rebels of the heart, rising
> in response to the mind's misguided
> perceptions and mental constructs. Honour
> them, but don't let them define you."

So here is the thing: we know that we are not our thoughts and feelings, and we know they are transient. Yet, why do we give them so much power? Why do we give them so much of our time? Why do we let them take us down rabbit holes of rumination, regret, guilt, and fear?

The truth is, we often neglect to truly understand, challenge, or even observe these fleeting thoughts and feelings. Instead, we allow them to enter our minds uninvited and wreak havoc. But it doesn't have to be this way.

The Ego & Divisions of the Mind

The purpose of this part of the book is to explore the divisions of the mind, so we can better understand how it's wired and learn to work with the brain rather than against it. None of these divisions actually exist in a way we can point to. We cannot consider them as we can an organ like the brain or heart.

The ego and divisions of the mind act as different layers of experience within the same, indivisible field of awareness.

The ego is what we refer to as the sense of self that we identify with. The ego is not inherently good or bad, just misinformed. The ego has a hard role in the play of life, receiving messages from various conflicting divisions of the mind.

Conscious Mind: The conscious mind encompasses all thoughts, perceptions, and experiences we are aware of in our everyday waking state. This includes our active thoughts, sensations, and the immediate environment we perceive through our senses.

Linked to the brain's prefrontal cortex (PFC), it processes higher cognitive functions like planning, decision-making, problem-solving, and impulse control.

Subconscious Mind: Our subconscious mind is the repository for all our accumulated life experiences and beliefs. Thoughts move from the nonconscious to the conscious here. It is "just aware", operating just below the level of conscious awareness, guiding much of our automatic behaviours, social conditioning and reactions. This is the mind we speak to during hypnosis. The subconscious does not know the difference between what is real and what is imagined. This is where most perceptual problems exist.

Nonconscious Mind: The primordial portion of the mind responsible for survival. It scans all information, is very powerful, and works 24/7. The nonconscious mind refers to processes and functions that are completely outside of conscious awareness and control, such as bodily functions (heartbeat, digestion, breathing) and deeply ingrained survival instincts.

How Humans Are Biologically Wired

Humans are biologically wired for survival through a complex set of physiological and psychological mechanisms evolved over millions of years, taking residency primarily in the nonconscious mind, which is outside of conscious awareness and therefore much harder for us to access. By understanding how these mechanisms function we can work with them rather than against them, the truth is they are too strong to resist. They are optimised for the challenges faced by our hunter-gatherer ancestors rather than the modern-day environment.

Let's look at just some of them that affect our cognitive style, in other words how they affect the way we think, our thought patterns.

Low Tolerance for Ambiguity: We do not like uncertainty. Uncertainty for our ancestors meant certain death, for example, if they didn't know where the next few days of food were coming from or where there was a safe place to sleep.

Cognitive Bias: We have a very powerful nonconscious bias that wants to be right. Linked to our intolerance for ambiguity, we are prediction machines, and cognitive bias looks for and recognizes evidence and patterns that support its prediction, allowing us to make quick decisions based on limited information. However, in the modern world, this can lead to misinformation and errors in judgement.

Low Tolerance for Discomfort: From an evolutionary perspective, avoiding discomfort was crucial for survival. We default to pleasure over pain, whether physical or psychological, without the cognitive recognition of foresight, which rationalises short-term discomfort or pain leading to long-term benefits.

Perpetual Dissatisfaction: This drive for improvement ensured that those who were never fully satisfied were more likely to adapt and thrive in changing environments. It is a catalyst for growth and adaptation, pushing us to continually evolve.

Negative Thinking: Catastrophes, gossip, and bad news make headlines because we are attracted to them. Bad news is more powerful at getting our attention than good news. So, we often default to creating internal storylines, catastrophizing events and situations rather than positive outcomes. Early humans needed to be constantly aware of potential dangers, such as predators or hostile environments. Negative thinking helped them remain vigilant and prepared for the worst-case scenarios.

These five very powerful instinctual mechanisms work very well with the ego to form your cognitive style. Perceiving itself to be a separate individual it will operate from this primordial prison. Catastrophizing uncertainty, looking for "proof" that it's right, overlooking facts, seeking comfort (usually unhealthy) from discomfort, never being satisfied and always imagining the worst-case-scenario. Sound familiar?

In my clinical practice, I often hear clients expressing struggles that arise from our biological wiring, which can lead to patterns that feel out of our control. Some common examples are:

- *"I can't seem to stop snacking at night, even though I'm not hungry."* This is often driven by our brain's need for comfort from discomfort, more on this later.

- *"Whenever I think about starting a new project, I get overwhelmed with anxiety and doubt which often leads to procrastination."* This is linked to the brain's instinct to avoid uncertainty and the unknown, a remnant of our ancestors' survival instinct.

- *"I keep putting off exercising, even though I know I feel better when I do it."*
  This can be a result of the brain's tendency to seek immediate pleasure and avoid the discomfort that can come with physical effort.

- *"I always assume people are judging me, even when they're not saying anything."*
  This response comes from our brain's heightened sensitivity to social threats, a mechanism evolved to keep us safe in social groups.

- *"I keep working late into the night, even though I'm exhausted, because I feel like I'm never doing enough."* This comes from our brain's drive for continuous improvement, which can turn into chronic dissatisfaction and burnout.

As you can see, we are not biologically equipped to deal with modern-day life, and commercialism has capitalised on this. Having immediate access to everything we could ever want to know in our pocket is making us even more adverse to uncertainty, doubt, and unpredictability.

Understanding The Way *You* Think

In psychology, "the way you think" is referred to as our cognitive style and it's shaped by the interplay of the different divisions of your mind: conscious, subconscious, and nonconscious.

These divisions influence how you perceive the world, where you focus your attention, how you relate to others, how you explain events, and how you learn.

Together, these factors form the unique lens through which you view and navigate life and just with any lens, it creates distortion. To better understand your cognitive style, let's dive into some key components.

Perception: Start by observing how you interpret the world around you. Do you typically see situations in a positive or negative light? Are you more attuned to details, or do you focus on the broader picture? Your perception reveals a lot about how you think.

Attention: Consider what consistently captures your attention. Do you naturally notice the positive aspects of situations, or do you find yourself focusing on potential problems? The things you attend to most often indicate whether your outlook is more optimistic or pessimistic.

Belief: Beliefs shape our lives; they are very important. If you believe you can do something, you will try. If you don't believe you can do something, you won't try. Beliefs are powerful enough to effect positive change. However, in many cases, they form unhelpful maps. Beliefs are generalisations or absolutes about the world, ourselves, and others. By nature, they lack distinction and evidence, tending to direct attention. Beliefs, by definition, are not truths; if they were truths, they would be facts. We cannot prove or disprove a belief. They become the scripts of our lives and determine our behaviour.

Most people are unaware of their cognitive style, they "think how they think" and that's them. Problems arise because "we don't know what we don't know", so if you don't recognize your cognitive style, especially when it causes distortion and drives unhelpful behaviour, changing it becomes incredibly difficult. However, once you become aware of your own style, you can begin to question and reshape it.

By experimenting with different styles of thinking, you may discover an approach that serves you better and once you start to experience these benefits you may want to begin challenging some of your beliefs.

Beyond Normal Limits

Research shows that our beliefs can profoundly impact our capabilities. Your thoughts and beliefs can release abilities beyond normal limits. For instance, psychologists Ulrich Weger and Stephen Loughnan discovered that people performed better on tests when they believed the correct answers were briefly shown on their screens, even when they weren't. This highlights how the expectation of knowing can enhance performance. I see this play out in my life, time and time again. If you and I ever get to meet, I will undoubtedly use my handstand journey as a metaphor for life, when I kick up into a handstand if I doubt my ability to balance I will surely fall, yet if I can gather the focus of my attention into a belief that I will kick up, catch my balance and stay there, then I usually do.

Professor Ellen Langer's studies at Harvard reveal even more about the power of belief. Her research on mindfulness and the "psychology of possibility" shows how our mindsets can influence our physical and cognitive health. One of her notable studies involved taking a group of men in their 70's and 80's placing them in a controlled environment. The men were instructed to live as they did twenty years ago, the environment mimicked the music, the decor, TV shows and newspapers of that era and they were even encouraged to address one another in the same way. Not just reminiscing about the past but actually embodying it. The men showed significant improvements in their health and vitality suggesting that mental states can dramatically impact physical outcomes. The study has had a profound impact on the fields of psychology, ageing, and health, challenging our assumptions about the limits of the human mind and body

Given this, it's clear that our perceived cognitive and physical limits are more flexible than we often realise. So, I invite you to question your existing beliefs, and I challenge you to create new ones. A close friend once said to me, "Jo, sometimes I think you live in 'cloud cuckoo land!'" To which I replied, "I do. I choose to, and it works just fine for me, my life is amazing, and I created it!"

I invite you to firstly question the beliefs that confine you, then, dare to reinvent them. Especially when societal norms push back, remember that embracing a fresh perspective can reveal capabilities beyond what you've ever imagined.

> *"Conformity is easy, but forging a new path can unlock your true potential, which is limitless, more on this later."*

Understanding why we operate the way we do, means we can do something about it. Overcoming cognitive distortions and negative thought patterns is where we break free from suffering.

Our skewed representation of reality, combined with conflicting information from the divisions of our mind dumped on an illusory, ill-equipped ego, gives us no doubt that unless we have tools to deal with this, we will spend our lives in despair and suffering.

Problems are born out of perceptual mistakes created by cognitive distortions. In other words, a pattern of negative thinking causes us to perceive reality in an inaccurate or exaggerated way creating unhelpful thoughts. One of my most memorable examples of this was my past fear of flying, for which I used to take diazepam. The *problem* was that whenever I began packing for a flight, I would become extremely anxious, so much so that I would self-medicate with a glass or two of alcohol. On the actual day of flying, I needed up to 10mg of diazepam.

The *perceptual mistake* was in believing the catastrophic story I had imagined as a result of my cognitive distortion (pattern of thinking), which went something like: "Packing for this trip is the last time I will see all my things; leaving home means I'll never see my cats again. Just after take-off, the pilot will realise there's a problem with one of the engines, the plane will break in half, and I will fall to my death. My family will relive my final moments for the rest of their lives." Dramatic, right? Not once did I pause to question the probability of that story, nor did I reflect on whether those thoughts were valid.

Looking back, I realise that there was a sense of anxiety within my family around the time of travel, which my subconscious must have absorbed. In an attempt to protect me, it concocted a blockbuster drama to keep me at home but it didn't work. Instead, I found a coping mechanism in drugs and alcohol.

We have somewhere between between 50,000 and 80,000 thoughts a day. In our awake state, we do not stop thinking. We can't possibly pay attention to every thought that enters our mind, so there is some sort of filter in place, which is in most cases subconscious. We are unaware of it. However, this means it's possible to manage the thoughts, so we need to bring awareness to them.

Key Takeaways

Attachment to Thoughts, Feelings, and Perceptions: Much of human suffering is rooted in our attachment to transient thoughts, feelings, and perceptions. Recognising these as temporary and not defining our true self can lead to inner peace and happiness.

Subjective Reality and Its Impact: We experience life through subjective interpretations shaped by our senses and individual perspectives. This subjective reality influences our judgments, emotions, and overall well-being.

Divisions of the Mind: Understanding the roles of the conscious, subconscious, and nonconscious minds helps us see how they influence our behaviour and perceptions. The conscious mind handles active thoughts and decision-making, the subconscious stores experiences and beliefs, and the nonconscious governs survival instincts and automatic biological functions.

Biological Wiring and Cognitive Styles: Humans are biologically wired with survival mechanisms that often conflict with modern life. These include low tolerance for ambiguity, cognitive biases, and a tendency toward negative thinking. Our cognitive style, shaped by these factors, influences our perception, attention and beliefs.

The Power of Belief: Beliefs play a crucial role in shaping our actions and attitudes. They are powerful enough to effect positive change but can also form limiting and inaccurate maps of reality. By understanding and challenging these beliefs, we can alter our behaviour and improve our mental state.

Understanding these concepts provides a foundation for addressing and transforming our state of mind.

POWERFUL TOOL:
Curiosity Compass – Navigate the Storm of Negative Rumination

Introduction

When trapped in negative thoughts, simply replacing them with positive ones often proves ineffective. Our biological wiring for negativity, a survival mechanism honed through human history, makes positive thinking alone insufficient. Instead, we harness the power of curiosity to break free from negative thought patterns. By engaging curiosity, you'll experience an immediate reduction in the emotional charge of problematic thoughts or feelings. It's nearly impossible to hold onto anger, sadness, regret, or worry while actively engaging your curiosity.

With the emotional charge reduced, we can run thoughts and feelings through a series of questions, to establish whether it's a helpful or unhelpful thought or feeling. When we are in the rumination loop we don't have clarity. With a fresh perspective we can then decide what action can be taken.

Preparation

This tool is intended for use when you need it; when you feel yourself overwhelmed or ruminating with unwanted thoughts and feelings, therefore there is little preparation required. You may write down your answers, although it's not a requirement for efficacy. This tool consists of three main parts. For an audio guide to practise with, scan the QR code provided.

The Practice

1. Observation

- Bring to mind a thought with a negative emotional attachment.

- Identify the emotion associated with this thought or scenario. Is it perhaps sadness, frustration, regret, anger, or guilt?

- Notice that you can observe this emotion – you are not the emotion itself.

- Recognize that you brought this thought and this emotion here. Isn't that interesting?

- Observe how engaging your curiosity has already begun to reduce the thought's power.

2. Validation

Ask yourself:

- Is this thought or feeling valid, is it real and true? Valid thoughts often lead to action or problem-solving.

- How do I know it's really true? Is it grounded in reality or driven by fear, speculation, or "what-ifs."

- What actual evidence do I have to support it? Do you have verifiable facts or experiences, not assumptions, stories or hypothetical scenarios?

If the thought isn't valid, or if you can't take positive action then the thought is not useful and is not serving you.

You will notice:

- It feels repetitive, with no resolution or new insight, you are looping back to the thought.

- It focuses on "Why did this happen?" or "What if it gets worse?"- questions that dwell on the past or future, not the present.

- Leaves you feeling stuck, anxious, or self-critical.

Important Note:

Not all difficult feelings need to be dismissed. Some emotions, like grief, sadness, or fear, are entirely valid responses to real-life situations, such as the loss of a loved one. These emotions are natural and healthy, they are expressions of love, connection, and meaning. In these cases, the goal isn't to push away or fix the feeling, but rather to *allow yourself to feel it fully.*

> *"When these emotions arise, give them the space they need to be experienced without judgement."*

Let yourself grieve, feel sadness, or honour the fear as a natural part of the human experience. However, notice when these valid emotions turn into unhelpful rumination. If the thought shifts into repetitive loops or "what-ifs" that cannot be resolved, this is when the practice can help you break free from unnecessary suffering.

3. Is the thought HELPFUL or UNHELPFUL?

- If the thought is valid, but you can't take positive action, it may still be important to honour the emotion. Allow it to be felt, but don't get lost in unproductive loops of thinking.

- If the thought is valid but you can't take action or find a resolution and you are drawn back into unproductive rumination loops, it's not serving you. It is not helpful – let it go.

- If the thought isn't valid, and you've found it's driven by fear, speculation, or "what ifs,". It is not helpful – let it go.

- If the thought is valid and you can take action, it's helpful – it's time to act.

- Is the thought helpful?

4. Taking Action or Letting Go

Taking Action on Helpful Thoughts: If you've decided to take action, do something immediately, even if it's just planning. Visualise positive action even if you can't do it right away. This takes you out of the rumination loop. This changes your story and invokes the power of momentum. If you can take action immediately, do it and move on.

Letting Go of Unhelpful Thoughts: If you've recognised the thought is unhelpful:

Visualise it as a ball you can mould in your hands, then wrap it securely in paper. With your strongest arm, imagine throwing it far into an ocean or deep ravine, watching it disappear from view. Shake your body—arms, shoulders, and torso—to release tension. Take a deep breath. Bring to mind five things you're grateful for, such as breath, a cup of tea, hot water, the sky, a loved one. Breathe deeply and remind yourself: "I am not my thoughts or feelings. I am free."

Conclusion

Curiosity is a powerful tool for reducing emotional charge so that we can effectively analyse the negative thought and break the cycle of rumination, moving towards positive action or powerful release.

Practise this tool regularly to answer the question I posed to you at the beginning of this Chapter: "how do you decide which thoughts to pay attention to and which ones to ignore?" Your reply now could be, "I use the curiosity compass."

The Case Of Magdalene

Magdalene is an artist, a mother of two teenage girls, and the wife of a high-performing CEO who was rarely home. She had a comfortable life that allowed her to paint while caring for her daughters. As she approached her late 40s, and her daughters prepared for university, she contacted me for support in deciding whether to save or end her marriage. She struggled with sleepless nights, racing thoughts, and fears of starting over.

Accustomed to financial freedom, she worried about earning her own income, how to sell her paintings, and her daughters' reactions. She also feared her husband's response or potential resistance to change.

Magdalene sought clarity, but what she needed were tools to navigate her uncertainties. The curiosity catalyst tool was pivotal in this journey. By observing her negative thoughts with curiosity, she reduced their emotional impact and began validating them. This process helped her separate fact from fiction; leading to either positive action or letting go of unproductive thoughts. Over the course of a year, she transformed her approach to challenges, built self-trust, and improved her decision-making and communication skills.

Ultimately, she did not separate from her husband. Instead, they learned to communicate and understand each other, designing a marriage that fulfilled their needs in new ways, which was very different from the marriage they unconsciously signed into as a result of social conditioning. Magdalene couldn't have planned this outcome but took it one step at a time, using curiosity whenever she worried or ruminated.

CHAPTER THREE

LOCUS OF CONTROL – EXTERNAL BLAME VS INTERNAL RESPONSIBILITY

"What keeps you trapped? Could it be blaming what can't be changed?"

Where Are You Placing Control?

In this Chapter, we'll explore why willpower falls short and introduce a powerful tool that will help you do what you say you want to do – by working with your brain, not against it.

This tool will enable you to end bad habits and create new ones, but not in the way you might expect. It's time to disrupt your thinking about control and change.

In the midst of life's challenges, the crucial question arises: do you hold the reins of control, or do you find yourself at the mercy of external forces? For us to make positive change, we must establish our locus of control.

Locus of control defines the degree to which individuals perceive control over events shaping their lives. It's essentially a belief system that distinguishes whether we believe outcomes result from personal actions (internal locus of control) or external circumstances (external locus of control). Seldom does one possess a 100% internal or external locus. Most individuals find themselves somewhere in between these extremes.

Characteristics of Internal Locus of Control

- Ownership of Actions: Takes responsibility for personal actions.

- Independence: Less influenced by others' opinions.

- Optimal Performance: Thrives when allowed to work at their own pace.

- Self-Efficacy: Exhibits a strong sense of self-efficacy.

- Goal-Oriented: Works diligently to achieve desired outcomes.

- Confidence: Faces challenges with confidence.

- Well-being: Demonstrates better physical health.

- Happiness: Reports higher levels of happiness and independence.

- Professional Success: Often attains greater success in the workplace.

Characteristics of External Locus of Control

- Blame Game: Attributes circumstances to external forces.

- Luck Factor: Credits luck or chance for successes.

- Helplessness: Feels incapable of changing situations independently.

- Hopelessness: Experiences a sense of hopelessness in challenging situations.

- Learned Helplessness: More susceptible to learned helplessness.

In my clinical practice, I often hear patients attributing their problems to external factors.

For example:
"Alcoholism runs in my family; it must be in my genes."
"My binge eating is a result of my controlling mother."
"I always date verbally abusive men because my dad was abusive to my mom, so I am following that pattern."
"I can't exercise the way I want to because I have to work."

These statements attempt to provide a "reason" for the problem, answering the "why" question. While this can offer some comfort and exoneration, it does not provide solutions. When you attribute a reason or an outside cause to your problem, you are giving away your power.

Let me emphasise that:

*"When you attribute a reason or an
outside cause to your problem, you
are giving away your power!"*

But what happens when we truly can't control what's happening in the outside world? When circumstances are beyond our scope for making change? We still have control over our inner world and how we respond to circumstances. Viktor Frankl provides us with a profound example of this resilience.

*"The ultimate freedom we have
is the freedom to choose our own
responses." – Viktor Frankl, Austrian
psychiatrist and Holocaust survivor.*

No matter what the world throws at us, it doesn't get to decide how we respond.

ZEN KOHEN – A Tale of Two Monks

A senior monk and a junior monk were travelling together. At one point, they came to a river with a strong current. As the monks were preparing to cross the river, they saw a very young and beautiful woman also attempting to cross. The young woman asked if they could help her cross to the other side.

The two monks glanced at one another because they had taken vows not to touch a woman.

Then, without a word, the older monk picked up the woman, carried her across the river, placed her gently on the other side, and continued with his journey.

The younger monk couldn't believe what had just happened. After rejoining his companion, he was speechless, and an hour passed without a word between them.

Two more hours passed, then three, finally the younger monk could contain himself no longer, he was furious, shocked and disappointed and blurted out, "As monks, we are not permitted to touch a woman, how could you then carry that woman on your shoulders?"

The older monk looked at him and replied, "Brother, I set her down on the other side of the river four hours ago. Why are you still carrying her?"

This simple Zen story illustrates how often we give our power to an external event, person or situation carrying around past hurts, holding onto resentments when the only person we are really hurting is ourselves.

When we get really honest with ourselves and look at where we place our locus of control, we may discover that we are putting a lot more control on the side of external circumstances. If we were to change our perception, our cognitive style and realise that we have a lot more control accessible to us internally, we find there are many things that we can do about a situation, and this profoundly influences our actions.

Challenging our social conditioning and existing beliefs, and taking responsibility for our thoughts, feelings, and behaviours reclaims our power and enables us to take action. Taking ACTION is where things really start to shift!

Feeling content wasn't good for the species!

A study published in the "Review of General Psychology" stated: "If satisfaction and pleasure were permanent, there might be little incentive to continue seeking further benefit or advances".

In Chapter Two, we explored our biological wiring and discussed how our low tolerance for discomfort and perpetual dissatisfaction were crucial for our ancestors' survival, acting as catalysts for growth, adaptation, and evolution. However, we now live in the safest, most well-educated, most democratic time in history.

Yet, the feeling of perpetual restlessness and dissatisfaction remains within us as a motivation for growth and expansion. We were given no manual, no guide on how to harness these driving forces for betterment. To gain access to our highest potential, we must figure this out for ourselves.

This tool, which I call 'The Disruptor,' will teach you how to work with your brain instead of against it, to let go of unhealthy habits, establish healthy ones, and connect with your own body intelligence. The more you use it, the stronger you get.

We constantly seek comfort from discomfort and have developed many coping mechanisms to deal with it. Most of these are unhealthy; some are fatal. Commercialism has exploited this wiring too. Many popular platforms such as Tik-Tok, You-Tube, Facebook and Instagram leverage users' desire for distraction or relief from boredom, often drawing on habit-forming techniques to keep people engaged offering escape from our daily drudgery in the form of shopping, celebrity gossip, unhealthy food and drink, or social-media interaction.

Overeating, alcohol abuse, binge-watching TV, porn, shopping, sleeping, gossiping all offer comfort from discomfort; a form of escapism and relief.

Anything that relieves discomfort is potentially addictive.

As a society, we are increasingly unable to pay attention, becoming more distracted and disconnected from our own body intelligence.

The motivation for diversion originates within us. As I write this, I am feeling the discomfort of my brain working. I am fighting the urge to Google a fact or phrase because I know that will lead me down the rabbit hole of distraction. I am thinking about having another cup of coffee and a biscuit. I'm tempted to look at my phone to see if there are any messages. All because it's "uncomfortable" to be sitting here writing. One skill I frequently share with my clients, and one I continuously practise myself, is the ability to embrace boredom, by recognising it, sitting with it, and allowing ourselves to become comfortably bored.

Why? Because two prominent psychological factors make satisfaction temporary and prompt us to distraction: boredom and hedonic adaptation.

Let's look at both of these.

BOREDOM is one of life's biggest discomforts. Our tolerance for boredom has decreased exponentially now that we can get the answer to any question within seconds. We have access to all kinds of entertainment at our fingertips and most of us can get any kind of food we desire delivered within the hour. We have the same day or next day online shopping. There is no limit to the solutions available to us to end our discomfort from boredom, most of them unhealthy and destructive.

A fascinating 2014 study published in "Science Daily" asked participants to sit in a room and think for 15 minutes. The room was empty except for a device they could use to mildly but painfully electrocute themselves. Prior to entering the room, the participants said they would happily pay to not be shocked. Yet, left alone with their own thoughts, 67% of men and 25% of women shocked themselves. The study concludes by saying: "People prefer doing to thinking. Even if it's so unpleasant they would normally pay to avoid it."

HEDONIC ADAPTATION is mother nature's bait and switch. In truth, I could write a whole book on this. In fact, there is one, "The Big Leap" by Gay Hendricks tackles this concept very well, describing "the upper limit problem" and why humans find it so hard to go beyond a zone of comfort and tend to self-sabotage when things are going really well, which keeps us from entering our zone of genius. Hedonic adaptation refers to the tendency to quickly return to a baseline level of satisfaction.

This low tolerance for discomfort and perpetual dissatisfaction prevents us from doing what we say we are going to do, leading to an unhealthy cycle.

In Chapter Two, we discussed the role of the subconscious as the repository for all our accumulated life experiences and beliefs. The subconscious does not distinguish between what is real and what is imagined. Operating just below the level of conscious awareness, it guides much of our automatic behaviours and reactions, forming the basis for habits, which are essentially "learned responses."

Habits are useful because they streamline decision-making, conserve mental energy, and automate behaviours, allowing us to efficiently navigate daily tasks and routines with minimal cognitive effort. They serve as energy savers, with 70% of our daily activities being habitual. We perform about one thousand habits every day, such as getting out of bed, walking around the house, and putting on our shoes. Ninety-five percent of these habits are useful, while five percent are not.

The good news is that we can learn new habits and unlearn existing ones.

Your Willpower Is A Lie, It's Sabotaging Your Life

Shocking, isn't it? We've been taught that with enough willpower, we can achieve anything. But what if I told you that relying on willpower alone is setting you up for failure?

A common mistake is believing the process of ending bad habits and introducing new good habits relies solely on determination and willpower. While this approach may work for some, most people need to be more strategic and outsmart the biological wiring of our brains so that it works with us, not against us.

To change our behaviour, we must alter the reward value assigned to behaviours in our brain's reward hierarchy. The orbital frontal cortex (OFC) collaborates with the prefrontal cortex (the cognitive brain) to assign a reward value to everything we do. This system was essential for our hunter-gatherer ancestors, who constantly tested new foods, places to sleep, and tools. If an experience was positive, a high reward value was subconsciously assigned, encouraging repetition. Conversely, negative experiences received low reward values, discouraging repetition.

Reward values are based on immediate rewards rather than long-term benefits. Commercialism exploits this brain feature by offering immediate and intense rewards through unhealthy food, social media, online shopping, and more.

This third tool will help you do what you say you want to do. It will help you break unhealthy habits that do not serve you and install new habits you choose to include in your life.

I would like to tell you about Abby before I introduce you to the tool.

The Case Of Abby

In her 20s, Abby was an active club swimming coach, always on her feet. By her early 30s, she relocated to the UK for a more sedentary role organising global club competitions, which soon became repetitive and boring. She started indulging in White Chocolate Mocha Frappuccinos and honey-covered shortbread for comfort, gaining weight and cutting down on her regular swimming sessions. Her social life diminished, and evenings were spent alone with wine and TV, leading to further weight gain and misery.

In 2022, at New Year, Abby decided it was time for change. Her initial willpower lasted only eight days. This cycle repeated for eight months until she sought my professional help. During our sessions, I introduced Abby to the A.T.L.A.S. tools, with a significant breakthrough coming from tool number three, "The Disruptor."

The Disruptor taught Abby to work with her brain's natural impulses rather than resisting them. She mapped her habit of drinking wine, noting when and why it occurred, and how it made her feel in the long term. She observed that the habit stemmed from boredom and led to feelings of sluggishness, guilt, and poor sleep.

We introduced a disruptor: elderflower tonic water with frozen berries to replace the wine. When the urge to drink arose, Abby observed the discomfort and used the curiosity compass tool to explore the validity of her feelings. She realised that the boredom was temporary and could be managed. By using the disruptor, she felt fresh, light, and proud – and her OFC's reward hierarchy was updated time and time again.

Through practice and patience, Abby broke her old habits and built new, healthier ones. She learned to pay attention to feelings that served her and let go of those that didn't, leading to a significant transformation in her life.

Key Takeaways

Understanding Locus of Control and Its Impact

Locus of control defines how individuals perceive the influence of their actions on the events in their lives. Those with an internal locus believe their actions determine outcomes, leading to greater independence, confidence, and success. Conversely, those with an external locus attribute outcomes to external factors like luck or other people, often feeling helpless. Recognising where one lies on this spectrum is crucial for personal growth and empowerment.

Personal Responsibility

When individuals attribute their problems to external factors, they give away their power and responsibility, limiting their ability to effect change. Shifting towards an internal locus of control empowers individuals to take responsibility for their thoughts, feelings, and behaviours, leading to significant positive changes. This shift is essential for breaking free from negative patterns and establishing healthier habits.

The Psychological Drivers of Behaviour: Discomfort and Adaptation

Human beings have a low tolerance for discomfort and a tendency for hedonic adaptation, meaning satisfaction from positive experiences is often temporary. This biological wiring leads to unhealthy coping mechanisms like overeating, alcohol abuse, and escapism through various distractions. Understanding these drivers helps in developing strategies to manage discomfort constructively, building resilience and creating lasting changes in behaviour.

Practical Application of "The Disruptor" for Habit Formation

The tool "The Disruptor" teaches individuals to work with their brain's natural tendencies rather than against them, facilitating the end of unhealthy habits and the creation of new, healthier ones. By altering the reward values assigned to behaviours in the brain's reward hierarchy, individuals can break free from the cycle of seeking immediate comfort from discomfort and instead focus on long-term benefits. This tool, combined with an understanding of the locus of control, empowers individuals to take actionable steps towards personal transformation and achieving their goals.

POWERFUL TOOL:
The Disruptor – Breaking Bad!

Introduction

Before we dive into the tool itself, take a moment to reflect on your own thought patterns. Connect with your true self, as we discussed in Chapter One. Find that inner space of peace and contentment, even if just for a few seconds.

Now, ask yourself: Where in your life are you attributing your actions to external causes? Are you blaming your job, family, spouse, finances, or health for not pursuing your goals? Are you taking responsibility for your internal dialogue?

As we've explored earlier, attributing your problem to an external cause is effectively giving away your power. Now, it's time to shift our focus to what is truly within our control and change what we have the power to change.

For an audio guide and additional resources, including habit-mapping examples and blank worksheets, scan the QR code provided.

Preparation

I invite you to choose an unhealthy habit you want to change, there is no need to rush. We'll start small to build confidence with the reward hierarchy and learn which feelings to pay attention to and which to ignore.

Now, if you want to follow along, choose your own unhealthy habit to work on. We'll use Abby's wine drinking habit as an example.

Habit Mapping

Instructions: Write down your answers to the following questions:

- When and where does this habit occur?

- What discomfort are you seeking comfort from?

- How does the habit make you feel in the long term?

Example – Abby's Notes: "I pour my first glass of wine around 6pm, at home. I'm bored; my work for the day is done, I want dinner, and I have about an hour to kill. Initially, the wine feels good but that only lasts about 10 minutes. Then, I feel sluggish and start snacking on crisps while making dinner. I usually drink two glasses before dinner, then have at least one more. I eat more than I need, feel full and bloated, don't sleep well, and wake up at night feeling guilty. The next morning, I have a headache, feel tired and heavy, and promise myself I won't drink today, only to find myself pouring another glass at 6pm."

Choose Your Disruptor

Prepare a disruptor to use when the urge to perform the habit arises. The key is to replace the bad habit with something else and plan for it.

Example: For Abby, we chose elderflower tonic water with frozen berries as a replacement for wine. If your habit is having dessert after meals, you might brush your teeth immediately after eating as a disruptor. If you find yourself snoozing through your alarm rather than waking up, you might try placing your alarm clock or phone on the other side of the room. This forces you to physically get out of bed to turn it off, which can break the cycle of repeatedly hitting the snooze button. Alternatively, try setting a morning intention the night before. I find that stretching whilst still in bed combined with breathing exercises is something I really enjoy and it gives me something positive to focus on upon waking. If you find yourself vaping during breaks from work, try replacing the urge with a quick physical reset; take a brisk walk, squeeze a stress ball, or do some light stretching while focusing on deep, slow breaths. This blend of movement and mindful breathing helps relieve stress and reduces cravings, offering a healthier outlet.

The Practice

When the urge to perform the habit arises:

- Notice it without fighting it.

- Tell yourself you can perform the habit later, giving it 10 minutes.

- Observe the discomfort and name it out loud (e.g., "I'm bored!").

- Get curious about the feeling. Ask yourself:
  - What does this feeling (e.g., boredom) feel like?
  - How intense does it become if I don't react?
  - What happens if I don't reach for my usual comfort?

- Use your prepared disruptor.

- Stay curious and let time pass.

7. Once the urge disappears, write down how the experience felt.

Example – Abby's Response: "Wine o'clock time! I can feel the urge to pour a glass of wine . . . pause. You can have wine later but wait at least ten minutes more. I can see the boredom, I can see how temporary it is, this is interesting. Jo asked me what life would look like without my wine habit, she asked what kind of person would have tonic instead? I will think about this to fill in my boredom gap. I poured tonic water, took a sip, and felt fresh, light, and proud. This evening is the first night in years that I have not had alcohol. I slept well, woke up feeling healthy, so very proud, motivated, and alive! This is what tonic looks like."

Practice and Patience

- Don't expect immediate results. Habits take time to build and time to break.

- You may succumb to old habits or fail to complete new ones for days or weeks.

- Keep repeating this tool to harness the power of momentum.

- Be consistent but not hard on yourself for failures.

- When you fail, write it down and stay curious about the feelings.

- Pay attention to feelings that serve you and let go of those that don't.

Remember, little by little, you can make great changes. Consistency is key. Every time your brain constructs an experience, it becomes easier to reconstruct it. We are prediction machines using past experiences to make predictions about the immediate future, which becomes our present.

You're doing great! Keep up the good work!

CHAPTER FOUR

ADVENTUROUS AWAKENING

"Your comfort zone is slowly killing you."

Do you even know what you are capable of, or are you too busy defending your limitations?

"Your comfort zone is slowly killing you."

I say that quite a lot. It's a bold statement, isn't it? Yet, as we explore the activities that shape our daily lives and the adventures that create new neural pathways, you'll come to understand why stepping out of your comfort zone is not just beneficial, it's essential for growth.

An adventurous awakening occurs when you push beyond your perceived limits. There are a few key elements that optimise this experience. First, let's clarify the distinction between fear and safety.

Fear is psychological; it stems from the stories we tell ourselves about worst-case scenarios. The truth is, 95% of the fears we create in our minds never come to fruition, so fear should never be the reason we hold back from pursuing what we desire. Safety, however, is different because there is psychological safety (a feeling) and physical safety (a practical assessment), which requires a real-world evaluation of risk. To distinguish between psychological and physical safety, we must evaluate risk by considering both what is possible and what is probable. When we take on something that frightens us, we should still expect to be physically safe; this means preparing properly and ensuring we have the right training and support. For example, scuba diving with a buddy is not advisable if you're not qualified to do so, just as climbing Kilimanjaro without sufficient training and support is unwise, so too is embarking on safaris with wild animals without experienced guides.

That said, for an adventurous awakening to be successful, we need to step far enough beyond our comfort zone to release adrenaline, elevate our heart rate, and boost circulation. In this space, there's a sharp sense of uncertainty because we don't know what will happen next. Our survival brain, having failed to stop us from taking the leap, can no longer effectively do its job, so it must quickly adapt. This expansion of the comfort zone creates new neural pathways, allowing us to catch up with what we're doing. As a result, we feel fantastic, and our confidence grows.

We all have this sense of adventure because our true nature seeks to experience what life has to offer. Our true nature isn't afraid, it's our cognitive mind that imposes limits. I've had the privilege of witnessing hundreds of adventurous awakenings, from children to adults in their eighties.

So, what could be your adventurous awakening? What have you longed to experience but held back from due to fear? Could it be snorkelling with sharks, solo travel, public speaking, learning to swim, joining a dance class, travelling the world, attending a yoga retreat, trekking the Himalayas, or entering a competition? If you fight for your limitations, you'll win. If you don't believe you can achieve something, you're probably right. I invite you to challenge these perceived limitations and do the things that scare you!

Your Inner Doctor

How we spend our days and nights, our activities, and our lifestyle dictate whether our mind and body achieve homeostasis. Homeostasis is the state of balance among all the body systems, which is needed for the body to survive and function correctly.

"Don't ask what the world needs, ask what makes you come alive and do that. Because what the world needs is for more people to come alive! " – Howard Thurman

Achieving this balance isn't about settling into comfortable routines. It's about challenging ourselves, pushing boundaries, and embracing the unknown.

We are inundated with information about what we should and shouldn't eat, what exercises to do at various ages, and how long we should do them.

We are constantly told what's toxic and what's not, the good and bad microbiomes, how long we should fast, what supplements to take, and the proper intake of proteins, macros, and micronutrients. It's overwhelming, I tend to avoid this constant feed of dos and don'ts . . . I need things simplified. How do we simplify it? We listen to our body instead of allowing ourselves to be bombarded with outside information.

First, let's look at why homeostasis is important.

When we are in homeostasis, our prefrontal cortex (PFC) and orbitofrontal cortex (OFC) are better positioned to send grounded and practical information rather than impulsive reactions to our survival brain. You may recall from Chapter Two that our survival brain is ancient and powerful, based on biological wiring that kept our ancestors alive. Working with the limbic system, the survival brain will generate emotional responses and quick, instinctual reactions that often serve short term over long term positive results.

The younger PFC and OFC handle complex cognitive behaviours such as planning and decision-making, which means they can evaluate longer term benefits over short discomfort, but they are no match for the survival brain in terms of speed and power. At best, the PFC and OFC function optimally when we are in homeostasis. It's therefore in our very best interest to maintain a state of balance.

Have you ever noticed that when you are tired, your emotional pendulum has a greater swing and you may crave sugar and unhealthy snacks? You may get 'hangry'. This is your survival brain driving behaviour, taking over when you are not in homeostasis, leading to more reactive and instinctual actions.

Our brain is just one organ that functions optimally in homeostasis. The truth is our entire human vessel requires this stability too. It's mind-blowing how terribly we take care of our bodies. I'm convinced that if we could regularly look inside to see what terrible shape they are in, we wouldn't do what we do to them.

It does not help matters that as a society, we haven't defined what "health" actually is. We have "health care," but when we examine what's provided, it's actually "sick care." We live our lives in a certain way until we get sick, then we might see a doctor who will likely prescribe medication to treat the symptoms. While I am not anti-medication and I'm very grateful to our medical teams when we are in need of help, there is often a more natural and holistic alternative to keeping ourselves metabolically healthy.

Often overlooked is the powerful inner doctor we all possess. This non-conscious biological intelligence we have been looking at drives survival, reactive and instinctual responses, and creates and maintains our entire body. And what's truly remarkable is our ability to communicate with this innate body intelligence. Learning to listen and respond to our inner doctor in homeostasis, we can achieve optimal health and well-being, potentially maintaining metabolic health well into our later years.

Our body intelligence is so powerful that when we ignore the signals, if we don't take the time to learn its method of communication, it finds ways to get our attention to stop us in our tracks. Disease, chronic health problems, addictions, depression, and anxiety often serve as warning signs that we're out of sync with our true nature. These are not just random occurrences but messages from our inner doctor, urging us to make changes. Our inner doctor has an intricate relationship with our true self.

In the following sections, we'll explore key activities that support homeostasis, setting the stage for a more profound connection with your body's innate wisdom. Remember, the goal is to work in harmony with your inner doctor, not against it. By aligning our lifestyle choices with our body's needs, we pave the way for improved health, greater resilience, and a deeper understanding of ourselves.

Activities to Stay in Homeostasis

Sleep: Sleep is never wasted time. "I'll get enough sleep once I'm dead" misses the point of sleep. "I only need four hours of sleep a night" will catch up with you one day. The non-conscious mind works 24/7, and at night, while our body and cognitive brain rest, night processes take place: recovery, repair, healing, regenerating, filing, organising, and disposing of information. Metabolic waste builds up during the day and gets flushed out at night. Most adults need between six to eight hours of sleep per night. Aim for the amount and quality of sleep that works best for you, maintaining a consistent sleep routine is key.

Nutrient Richness & Hydration: I like to keep things simple. Studies show that eating whole foods like fruits, vegetables, whole grains, nuts, and seeds, and staying properly hydrated promote weight loss, reduce calorie intake, and improve digestion and satiety. This supports overall health and longevity by building a stronger immune system and reducing nutrient deficiencies. Whole foods refer to food consumed in its natural state or as close to it as possible, with minimal processing or refinement. Training yourself to buy only these foods is a game-changer. Consider processed food as not food! The idea behind whole foods is to retain natural nutrients and avoid losing essential vitamins, minerals, and fibre during processing.

Frequent Movement & Baseline Level of Fitness: Early humans were nomadic heterotrophs, relying on movement to find food sources. Our genetic code realised that movement happens frequently throughout the day, creating synergies between internal movement and body functions, in other words our body literally uses muscle contractions to run daytime biological processes to keep us healthy.

Once you begin connecting with your body intelligence, she will tell you how to move. I'm not suggesting a specific fitness regime; plenty of experts do that.

However, for a baseline incorporating these four areas of fitness create a beautiful holistic approach:

- Muscular Strength: Your ability to lift heavy objects. Incorporating strength training exercises, like lifting weights, using resistance bands, or body weight exercises, helps build muscle mass, increases metabolic rate, supports joints, and improves bone density. This is essential, especially as we age.

- Muscular Endurance: Your ability to maintain a strength exercise over a longer period.

- Cardiovascular Endurance: The ability of your heart and lungs to deliver oxygen to your organs at a faster pace. Running, HIIT training, cycling, and brisk walks are ideal. This ability also increases your energy levels.

- Mobility: Your ability to move your body around your joints. Yoga and Pilates are great. Squats and light resistance bands can also help.

To break up a sedentary day, do some micro-movements. Research suggests taking 10-minute breaks from sitting at the computer at least every 90 minutes. You might want to dance, shake your body, do hip rotations, squats, push-ups, or a sun salutation set. Anything to move your body, get your joints moving, and muscles contracting.

Deep Social Connection: We are social animals. Throughout human history, isolation was considered torture and often meant certain death. Solitary confinement in prison is punishment. A meta-analysis of 70 studies involving over 3.4 million people found that loneliness and social isolation increase the risk of early mortality by 26% and 29%, respectively. Social isolation is strongly linked to mental health issues such as depression and anxiety. It's crucial for maintaining cognitive function, especially in older adults. Regular social engagement reduces the risk of cognitive decline and dementia.

Interestingly, a study by Bruce Lipton, PhD, found that cancer cells grow more rapidly when isolated in a petri dish due to the lack of regulatory signals from surrounding cells in a living organism. This highlights the importance of connection and interaction for healthy cellular function.

Close friends, family, romantic partners, and communities can provide deep and meaningful connections. There is a tendency to believe that a single partner should fulfil all emotional and psychological needs, but this is often unrealistic and unhealthy. You may choose to have different connections to meet different needs while maintaining transparency and loyalty. For example, a friend might provide camaraderie and shared interests, while a family member offers unconditional love and historical connection. A romantic partner can offer intimacy and companionship, while a community provides a sense of belonging and shared purpose.

Having a diverse support network helps distribute the emotional load and can lead to more fulfilling and resilient relationships.

Sync with Nature: Our physical body needs its environment. We need sunlight, gravity, fresh air, and colour. Observing the effects on humans returning from outer space highlights the importance of our environment. Our need to sync with nature is not purely physical.

In Chapter One, we discussed the awareness of our true nature and our shared being with everyone and everything. There is an appearance of multiplicity and diversity, but behind the illusion of separation lies wholeness.

At our deepest level, everyone and everything is connected. We are nature. Life is something nature is doing; we are something that nature is doing.

Connecting with nature brings energetic balancing, grounding, fulfilment, and nurturing reassurance, stepping aside from our apparent separate self. Appreciating nature's boundless power and awe and connecting with it as one infinite being allows us to realise our place in nature and our part in something much bigger than us. Many of us know that being in nature feels good – a walk in the woods, witnessing a beautiful sunset, swimming in the ocean – we sense the shift and fulfilment. Yet, most of us remain oblivious to just how powerful that feeling is and how, through nature, we can become limitless and complete. We'll discuss this more in Chapter Five.

"We delight in the beauty of the butterfly, yet rarely admit the changes it has gone through to achieve that beauty." – Maya Angelou

Key Takeaways

Adventurous Awakenings

They happen when you push past your perceived limits and face your fears, while still maintaining a sense of safety through preparation. Fear is often based on imagined outcomes that rarely occur, so it shouldn't prevent you from pursuing what excites you. By stepping into uncertainty, you create new neural pathways, boosting confidence and expanding your comfort zone. Challenge your perceived limitations and embrace the experiences that scare you to truly grow.

The Importance of Homeostasis

Homeostasis is essential for the optimal functioning of both the mind and body. It ensures that all bodily systems (including the prefrontal cortex (PFC), orbitofrontal cortex (OFC), and survival brain) work efficiently. When in homeostasis, our cognitive functions, emotional responses, and instinctual behaviours are balanced, contributing to overall health and wellbeing.

Lifestyle Recommendations for Homeostasis

- **Sleep**: Adults need six to eight hours of quality sleep per night to allow for recovery, repair, and metabolic waste removal.

- **Nutrient Richness & Hydration**: Consuming whole foods and staying hydrated help to support overall health and reduce nutrient deficiencies.

- **Frequent Movement & Fitness**: Regular physical activity, including strength training, cardiovascular exercise, and mobility workouts, are essential for maintaining health.

- **Deep Social Connections**: Strong social ties reduce the risk of mental health issues and improve overall wellbeing.

- **Sync with Nature**: Regular interaction with natural environments provide physical and mental health benefits.

The Concept of the Inner Doctor

The body has an innate intelligence within the non-conscious mind that maintains and heals it. Learning to communicate with this inner intelligence reveals what our mind and body needs. This leads to better health and wellbeing, allowing individuals to live healthier lives well into old age.

POWERFUL TOOL:
Body Intelligence – Listening to Your Inner Wisdom

Introduction

> *"Our body intelligence orchestrates the creation and development of our physical form, beginning with the intricate process of embryonic growth. It knows what we need, yet we don't ask for its guidance. We have forgotten how to communicate"*

Let me introduce you to your own body intelligence. Use the QR code below to practise with audio.

Preparation

- Find a quiet, comfortable space where you won't be disturbed.

- Sit or lie down in a position that allows your body to fully relax.

- Take several deep, slow breaths to centre yourself.

The Practice

- Close your eyes and bring your awareness to your body.

- Starting from your toes, slowly scan upwards. As you scan, release any tension you encounter:

- Feel your feet, ankles, calves, knees, thighs.

- Notice your hips, lower back, abdomen, chest.

- Be aware of your fingers, hands, arms, shoulders.

- Sense your neck, face, and the top of your head.

- Turn your awareness inward, beyond your physical sensations.

- Observe your thoughts and feelings without judgement.

- Recognise that these mental states are transient, flowing through you.

The Heart Vortex Visualisation

- Focus your attention on your heart centre.

- Visualise a swirling vortex of energy here. Choose a colour that resonates with you – green or white are common choices – but trust your intuition.

- Imagine this vortex spinning, drawing out:
  - Negative energy
  - Limiting beliefs
  - Uncomfortable emotions
  - Physical discomfort

- See these being dispersed and transmuted into neutral energy. Spend as long as you need here (30-90 seconds might be comfortable).

- Now, reverse the vortex. Visualise it drawing in:
  - Vitality
  - Clarity
  - Wellbeing
  - Positive energy

- Spend as long as you need here (again, 30-90 seconds might be comfortable).

Listening to Your Body

- With the vortex gently spinning, ask your heart centre: "What do I truly need right now?"

- Stay open to whatever arises: images, words, sensations, or emotions.

- Don't analyse or judge. Simply observe and accept the first impression you receive.

Integrating the Experience

- Gradually let the vortex slow and fade.

- Take a moment to appreciate the wisdom of your body.

- Mentally express gratitude for this communication.

- Slowly wiggle your fingers and toes, gently stretching as you return to full awareness.

Reflection and Action

- Over the next few days, reflect on the message you received.

- Consider how you can honour what your body is asking for.

- What small steps can you take to address this need?

Remember, this is a skill that deepens with practice. The more you listen and respond to your body's wisdom, the clearer and more profound the communication will become. Be patient and consistent in your practice.

As you work to implement changes based on your body's guidance, refer back to "The Disruptor" tool to help break old patterns and establish new, supportive habits.

Your body holds deep wisdom. By learning to listen and respond, you're embarking on a transformative journey of self-discovery and holistic well-being.

The Case Of Ian

Ian, a 65-year-old CEO, initially came to me seeking help to reduce his daily wine consumption. Whenever someone presents an unhealthy habit or dependency (addiction) it's never about the "thing". The "thing" is the coping mechanism, the comfort from discomfort. Sure enough, as we delved deeper, it became clear that Ian's issue wasn't about alcohol, it was about purpose.

Despite running a successful company, Ian felt bored and uninspired. His social drinking had increased, leading to weight gain and decreased energy.

Using the Body Intelligence tool, Ian sensed a growing urge to find his tribe.

Puzzled but intrigued, Ian followed this cryptic message. It led him to discover a group that combined outdoor adventures, personal growth, and surprisingly, flying lessons. Initially sceptical, Ian decided to give it a try. The experience was transformative. He found himself tackling new challenges, engaging in meaningful conversations, and even taking his first flying lesson.

The results were transformative. Through the group, Ian made new friends who prioritised healthy living. He was challenged, taken out of his comfort zone, and introduced to new adventures. Unexpectedly, he discovered a passion for flying.

Ian's journey illustrates a crucial point: often, what we perceive as a specific problem (like excessive drinking) is a symptom of a deeper need. By tuning into his body's wisdom and embracing new challenges, Ian not only addressed his initial concern but also rediscovered purpose and vitality in his life. His story reminds us that it's never too late to reinvent ourselves and find new sources of meaning and joy, even after achieving outward success.

CHAPTER FIVE

SENSE OF ABUNDANCE
– PASSIVE LIFE VS
INTENTIONAL LIFE

What if tapping into nature could manifest your greatest desires?

Shifting from Pursuit to Alignment

Finding purpose has been a source of both inspiration and anxiety for many. While studies show that people with a sense of purpose tend to live longer and take better care of themselves, the pursuit of purpose has become an industry in itself, often leading to feelings of inadequacy or anxiety. But what if our purpose in life is much more accessible than we've been led to believe?

Reflecting on our conversation from Chapter One about the interconnectedness of all things, let's now broaden this understanding to the entire universe. What if universal consciousness expresses itself through nature, through all living beings, through us? Can you see what that means?

If we are indeed an expression of one infinite consciousness, then we are not limited, we are boundless, infinitely powerful, and complete. We are abundance itself, an integral part of the universe's ever-expanding creative force. Imagine living from that realisation.

When you begin to view life through this lens, your entire world transforms. Instead of seeing life as a battle, a place of scarcity and separation, you start to perceive it as abundant and flowing, everything happening just as it should. You slow down and allow space for inspiration and serendipity.

Opening up to this perspective, you start to see nature, animals, and people differently. The boundaries between yourself and the world dissolve, and judgement loses its grip on you. Forgiveness and acceptance come easier, and you become more compassionate, seeing yourself reflected in others.

This doesn't mean you no longer need to set goals and habits. You absolutely do. However, when we shift from striving and scarcity to a state of abundance, we recognize that goals are not about the future; they're about embodying that vision in the present.

I am very goal driven, I work well with structure, yet within that structure I make space for flow, I make space for silence, so I may receive and understand the messages. My process involves setting long-term goals: six months-to-three years and breaking them down into daily actions with regular accountability. The difference between living from what the future might bring, to the feeling you have right now, in the present moment is profound. When you live from wholeness, from the real-isation that you are already enough, your energy aligns with the infinite. The universe responds, not to the need, but to the invitation of your limitless potential.

I'm going to say that again in case you missed it.

"The universe responds, not to the need, but to the invitation of your limitless potential".

There will still be turbulence to deal with, this is not a Disney movie, you will still face challenges, you remain human!

However, this understanding does offer a new perspective with which to see your challenges and your trauma. The universe will show you where you are not free by presenting you with people and situations that trigger you; these can be seen as access points, a place from which we can explore. If you are consistently attracting the same problems, the same people, the same circum-stances then pay attention, look at them, what are they trying to teach you?

It may take a while, years, or decades to learn your lesson but when you do, the insight can immediately be life changing. My own journey was lengthy, yet my lesson was quite simple: release judgement. Stop judging others, stop judging myself and most importantly stop negating judgement by sacrificing my needs. Authenticity, slow down, heal and trust were words that kept showing up during my "Body Intelligence" practise.

I learned to show up authentically to myself and others; to be able to accept and rest in the space of disappointing and being judged by others. When I realised this lesson and began living from this understanding I stepped into my own empowerment. The tools of A.T.L.A.S have been – and continue to be – my everyday superpowers.

The Case Of Marina

When I first met Marina, I was instantly struck by admiration for her accomplishments. She was a single mom to a wonderful young boy, had a fantastic relationship with her son's father, and enjoyed a great career in central London. Beyond her professional life, she was an accomplished runner with multiple amateur wins and took great care of herself. Life appeared to be going well for Marina.

However, despite these achievements, she felt she was not living a life she had consciously created but rather one that had defaulted upon her. She had a strong sense that there was something else she wanted, there was a yearning.

When someone has this sense, it's wise to listen and explore. So, we did. I asked Marina about what she loved doing as a child. We delved into her childhood days, her favourite activities with her son, her travels, and the types of films she adored. I can always tell from a person's eyes when they start to align with their true nature and speak from this place, it might be high-level pattern recognition or pure intuition, I can see, feel and sense them light up from within.

During our conversations, it became evident that Marina had a passionate ambition to write fiction novels centred around dynasty families spanning generations. Occasionally, she would vividly narrate tales of family feuds lasting through the ages, and romantic stories of how two teenagers met, fell in love, married, and had children, whose descendants would grow into explorers. Her imagination was captivating. At any given moment, she carried within her the potential for at least two trilogies, weaving intricate, multi-generational sagas effortlessly.

As she created, her eyes sparkled, and her whole body came alive as she shared her character ideas. She felt it, and so did I. "But how am I going to find the time to create these novels? Should I sell them? I couldn't possibly make any money from this – could I?"

When people start focusing on logistics, I slow them down. Logistics activate the cognitive brain, triggering planning and reasoning. The survival brain is alerted to potential change and ambiguity and the primordial mental prison that we have constructed for ourselves will prepare its army for defence. It will use fear to halt us. It recruits limiting subconscious beliefs and actively seeks "evidence" to validate them. As a result, we begin noticing and attracting obstacles that extinguish our passion, all in the name of keeping us "safe."

At this early stage, when we connect with our deepest desires, it's almost impossible to know *how* to achieve them. The *how* comes later. For now, it's about creating space for dreams to surface and aligning with the universe's infinite creativity and expansion, so individuals can express and speak into the world their unique contributions.

I worked with Marina for just over a year. She stayed at her job while completing a creative writing course. Confident that her internal compass was pointing her in the right direction to fulfil her desire for writing, she used the tools of A.T.L.A.S daily. Challenging beliefs, validating thoughts and feelings, distinguishing between the ones that serve her and compartmentalising those that don't. She took responsibility for her actions, allowing others to have their opinions without judgement. Her commitment was admirable.

Fast-forward two years, she now collaborates with other writers to publish short stories, and earlier this year, her writing captured the attention of a prominent publisher. Impressed by her unique voice, they approached her with an exciting proposal.

Time and time again, I witness this sort of magic happening. Regular people realising their wildest dreams in unconventional ways, dissolving limiting beliefs, connecting and listening to their body intelligence, trusting in themselves, repeatedly experiencing their potential resting in fulfilment and abundance.

But how, you may wonder. Surely, at some point there must be a logistics conversation, we don't just say what we want and magically get it, right?

You're absolutely correct; there's more to this process. We need to prepare the individual for transformation, equipping them with the mindset and tools to navigate the challenges ahead. This preparation is essential for meaningful, lasting change. Read on to uncover how this journey unfolds and how the steps align to bring your desires into reality.

As you fully embrace this understanding, something magical occurs; nature begins to work through you. Your desires are fulfilled effortlessly, not because you chase after them, but because you allow them to manifest through you. In this state, you become an integral part of the universe's grand design to create, expand and express. Imagine the infinite possibilities this opens up, what could you create, expand, or express, knowing that unlimited potential is available to you?

When we truly grasp our oneness with all beings and the universe, our thoughts, actions, and relationships naturally align with love, peace, and abundance. We become vessels through which greater intelligence expresses kindness, understanding, and love into the world.

By aligning with this universal flow of creation and expansion, our dreams and goals become magnified. Helpful people appear at the perfect time, opportunities arise, and life feels as though it's working in our favour. What might seem like magic is simply the natural result of living in harmony with our true nature.

> *"Your purpose, then, isn't something external to be found; it's within you, waiting to be expressed. Once you recognize this, the pressure to "find" purpose falls away, and you begin to live it joyfully and effortlessly."*

Your mission is simple yet profound: explore what lights you up, what excites you, then do that, expand on that. Pursue your passions from a place of abundance, knowing that you are a unique expression of infinite consciousness.

This isn't just theory. I've drawn from the wisdom of the greatest philosophers and thinkers of our time and those before them, you will have noticed a beautiful collection of quotes from these masterful teachers within the book.

Now, I invite you to explore your own beliefs and harness the powerful tool of "The Pathless Path" bringing your inner world into alignment with the life you wish to create. Prepare to unfold your wings and get ready for the journey of a lifetime!

Key Takeaways

Trust Your Intuition: Marina's story emphasises the importance of listening to your inner yearnings and exploring what truly excites you. Often, the path forward is found by revisiting childhood passions or reflecting on what lights you up and excites you in the present.

Dissolve Limiting Beliefs: Limiting beliefs and fears naturally arise when you focus on logistics too soon. By slowing down and separating what serves you from what doesn't, you open space for creative potential to emerge.

Abundance Through Alignment: When you align with the universe's expansive creative force, obstacles dissolve, and the need to control outcomes fade. Goals become present realities rather than distant pursuits, allowing fulfilment to flow more easily.

Challenges Are Inevitable: People and situations that keep showing up in our life presenting challenges are here to teach us lessons and reveal where we are not free, we can use these opportunities to reflect on our subconscious beliefs and what we might need to let go of for growth and empowerment.

Embodied Purpose: Living your purpose isn't about searching outside of yourself but expressing the abundance that already exists within. When you align with universal consciousness, the boundaries between you and the world dissolve, and your unique contribution can manifest effortlessly.

How do you know you're on the right path? Because it disappears.

POWERFUL TOOL:
The Pathless Path – Unfold Your Wings

Information

This paradox reveals a profound truth: our finite minds cannot fully map out our journey. To find our true path, we must let go of perceived limitations and allow our authentic nature to guide us.

Preparation

- Find a quiet, comfortable space where you won't be disturbed.

- Prepare a journal or paper and pens for writing.

- If you're driving or engaged in an activity requiring attention, return to this exercise later.

- For an audio guide, scan the QR code provided.

The Practice

Part One: The Three Selves Exercise

This powerful tool helps you connect with different aspects of yourself to reveal some passions that will begin to light you up.

1. Past Self

- Close your eyes, relax, and breathe comfortably.

- Think back to moments of pure joy in your childhood, even if it was challenging, there were likely moments of joy and freedom.

- Ask yourself: What activities made you lose track of time? What made you feel alive? How did you play?

- Visualise these moments, reconnecting with your innate sense of playfulness, wonder and passion.

- Allow these positive memories and feelings to resurface fully and spend time here.

2. Future Self

- Now, imagine yourself five years into the future, living a life aligned with your deepest joy.

- What are you doing that brings you fulfilment? How are you contributing to the world?

- Where are you? Who surrounds you? How do you feel?

- Be curious and ask your future self questions about this joyful life. What did you let go of to get here?

- Allow impressions, words, or images to flow freely – there's no right or wrong way to perceive this.

- Your future self may communicate through feelings, visual snapshots, or even a sense of knowing.

3. Present Self

- Slowly open your eyes, remaining calm and centred.

- Write down everything you experienced, felt, or realised during this journey.

- Look for common threads or themes across your past joy and future fulfilment.

- Reflect on what these insights might reveal about your unique gift or purpose.

Practise this exercise regularly, allowing time for your subconscious to process and reveal deeper insights. The information may come gradually or in a sudden moment of clarity. Quite often insights or realisations come to you in your dreams, write them down and when repeating this exercise ask questions about your insightful dreams. Trust the process and remain open to unexpected revelations.

Part Two: Creating Your Ideal Day

Once you've completed the Three Selves Exercise and allowed time for insights to emerge, whether it takes moments, days, or weeks, you're ready to envision your ideal day. This visualisation will help you explore how you might integrate your newfound insights into your daily life.

- Find a comfortable, undisturbed place to sit.

- Close your eyes and take deep breaths, scanning your body to relax. Slightly turn up the corners of your mouth.

- Now, imagine your ideal day from the moment you wake up:
  - Visualise your bedroom and how you start your morning.
  - Consider your surroundings, the people present, and the sounds you hear.
  - Visualise your home, its location, and the view from your windows.

- How do you spend your first hour? Do you exercise, journal, or have breakfast?
- Imagine your work environment. What does your day's work entail?
- Visualise your lunch, afternoon activities, and evening routine.
- Take time to go into great detail.

- As you construct this ideal day, reflect on the revelations from part one:
  - In what ways can you align your day's activities with the vision of your future self?
  - Where can you create space for the unique gifts or purposes you've uncovered?

- Include rich details in your visualisation:
  - Engage all your senses: What do you see, hear, smell, taste, and feel?
  - Imagine the emotions you experience throughout this ideal day.
  - Consider how you interact with others and your environment.
  - Think about how you balance work, leisure, and personal growth.

- Dream big, approaching this exercise from a place of

abundance and possibility. Remember that your true nature is abundant and lacking nothing.

After visualising, gently return to the present moment. Reflect on your ideal day and how it might serve as a canvas for creativity, expansion and expression.

Be grateful for this vision without yearning for it. Instead, consider how you can begin to align aspects of your current day with elements of your ideal day. Integration is very important because if you are always dreaming about your ideal day, you will forever be dreaming about it. Bring as much of it into your current day and the present moment.

Revisit this visualisation regularly, allowing it to evolve as you continue to gain insights about yourself. Focus on the positive feelings it evokes, as these emotions can guide you towards making choices that align with your true self.

Remember, this is a process of exploration and integration. Your ideal day may change as you grow and discover more about yourself. Approach life with an open mind, avoiding feelings of limitation, grateful for your teachers that appear at first as challenges. Trust in the process and remain receptive to the infinite possibilities that await you on your pathless path.

A.T.L.A.S

TRUST THE JOURNEY
BEYOND THE MAP

As we reach the conclusion of this book, my sincere hope is that the powerful tools presented here, rooted in philosophy and blended with strategic psychotherapy, have been effectively translated from a clinical environment to empower you on your journey. These tools are designed to help you navigate the complexities and challenges of life and connect with different powerful aspects of yourself.

By practising these tools daily, you'll discover that they become stronger, empowering you to handle life's difficulties with greater ease. These quick exercises, taking just 2-3 minutes, can be practised individually or together, offering flexibility in their application.

Through my own experiences and those of my clients, I've witnessed time and time again the transformative power of A.T.L.A.S. tools.

With consistent practice, you'll find yourself better equipped to cope with challenges. You'll notice that fewer situations have the power to unsettle you, and you'll develop the ability to break free from rumination loops.

Changing your patterns and habits will become less daunting, and you'll become more attuned to your body's needs, whether it's related to food, movement, purpose, community or other aspects of life. You'll find that people and circumstances align to support your journey.

The exercises here are more than just tools, they are invitations to freedom. With time, patience, and consistent practice, you will discover that you are no longer confined by the limitations of past mental constructs or the unconscious patterns that have shaped and imprisoned you until now. By applying these principles, you begin to consciously create a wonderful life, stepping into the infinite potential of who you truly are. The future is yours to design, choose it with intention, and let each moment reflect the life you were always meant to live.

Moonlight A Study at Millbank.

This image is for illustrative purposes only and does not represent the original due to copyright restrictions.

Turners Moon

J.M.W. Turner's "Moonlight, A Study at Millbank," painted in 1797, is a captivating depiction of the River Thames at night as viewed from Millbank in central London.

What's particularly fascinating about this oil painting is the luminosity of the moon and its golden reflection on the water. Yet, upon closer inspection, one realises that Turner did not actually paint the moon. What we perceive as the moon is the only portion of the canvas that remains untouched—pure canvas.

This untouched segment serves as a profound metaphor. The unpainted, pure canvas, existing before any layers of oil, colour, boats, trees, or fishermen were applied, offers a window into the essence of the painting. This is "you"—the true self—before layers of conditioning, beliefs, thoughts, and feelings have been applied. Turner understood that this untouched part of the painting was its meaning and purpose, the portal through which the pure essence of the canvas is revealed.

Similarly, within each of us lies such a portal, an essential space untouched by the layers of our experiences and conditioning. This inner space is unlimited and infinite, a connection to our true, unconditioned nature. Just as Turner left the moon as pure canvas to reveal the essence of his painting, we can connect with this inner portal to create, expand and express. The purpose of life is to experience the boundless essence of our own being.

REFERENCES:

1. *Spira, R. (2021). You Are the Happiness You Seek: Uncovering the Awareness of Being. Sahaja Publications.*

2. *Weger, U., & Loughnan, S. (2013). The illusion of control by the illusion of control: When self-affirmation alters causal attributions. Consciousness and Cognition, 22(1), 173-176. doi:10.1016/j.concog.2012.11.003*

3. *Langer, E. (2009). Counterclockwise: Mindful Health and the Power of Possibility. Ballantine Books.*

4. *Wilson, T. D., Reinhard, D. A., Westgate, E. C., Gilbert, D. T., Ellerbeck, N., Hahn, C., . . . & Shaked, A. (2014). Just think: The challenges of the disengaged mind. Science, 345(6192), 75-77. doi:10.1126/science.1250830*

5. *Holt-Lunstad, J., Smith, T.B., & Layton, J.B. (2010). Social Relationships and Mortality Risk: A Meta-analytic Review. PLOS Medicine, 7(7), e1000316.*

6. *Cacioppo, J.T., & Cacioppo, S. (2018). Loneliness in the Modern Age: An Evolutionary Theory of Loneliness (ETL). Advances in Experimental Social Psychology, 58, 127-197.*

7. *Leigh-Hunt, N., Bagguley, D., Bash, K., Turner, V., Turnbull, S., Valtorta, N., & Caan, W. (2017). An Overview of Systematic Reviews on the Public Health Consequences of Social Isolation and Loneliness. Public Health, 152, 157-171.*

8. *Donovan, N.J., & Blazer, D. (2020). Social Isolation and Loneliness in Older Adults: Review and Commentary of a National Academies Report. American Journal of Geriatric Psychiatry, 28(12), 1233-1244.*

www.HansahLife.com

Printed in Great Britain
by Amazon

58303976R00086